Devotionals from the Barn

Inspiration from Horses

Table of Contents

Dedicated to the God who unconditionally loves and looks after me and to all the amazing and wonderful four-legged friends that he placed in my life...

Queenie
Toby
Shadow
TC
Scooter
Hickory
Ringo
Cheyenne
Autumn
Riona
Cadence
and so any more....

Who would I have been without you?

OTHER BOOKS BY KAYLA PETERS

Massage Therapy Business Success

The Chocolate Lover's Cookbook

Booked Up: Marketing Your Business with Chair Massage

INTRODUCTION

As a child I had the privilege of growing up on a small third generation family farm, which meant I got to spend long summer days riding in tractors, ripping around our massive yard with my pink Barbie bike, helping Grandma weed the garden, and playing with baby animals.

Many people find the prairie landscape plain and boring but in my mind, nothing is as beautiful as a ripe wheat field with a sunset behind it. There is a quiet, peaceful solitude that can't be found anywhere else. My childhood home was built on the top of a ridge-like hill and as a small child, I spent many hours surveying the expansive view from our living room window. It overlooked miles and miles of grain, canola, and hay fields with an elevator off in the distance. When I close my eyes I can still picture it just as it was all those years ago. I loved to stand outside on a windy day, spread my arms and imagine that they were wings and I was flying.

But the best part of it all was the horses! Not only am I a third generation farmer's wife, I am also a third generation certified horse fanatic. My grandfather used horses to work the land when he was young and told many colorful stories about those days. When horses were no longer necessary to work the land, they stayed on as companions and eventually he purchased purebred breeding stock.

My mother loved horses as much as he did and she spent many years breeding and showing top quality bloodlines. When her health prohibited her from being that involved the horses still stayed, but weren't used as regularly.

It came as no small surprise to me when at my wedding my father stood up and told the story of me coming home from the hospital. Apparently, Mom brought me home and only a few short hours later bundled me up to take me on my first real outing, a horse show.

As a little girl, my Grandma explained to me that there is no place on earth as close to God as a garden. This thought confused me for a long time as I was sure that she was wrong.

In my mind, there can be no place on earth that is closer to God than on the back of a horse.

WHY YOU SHOULD READ THIS BOOK

There's something therapeutic about the velvety feel of a horse's nose, and the way that they nicker to you when you step into the pasture. These beautiful creatures never cease to amaze me with their intelligence and grace.

The same horse can both frustrate and thrill me in a matter of a few minutes, but there is no place in the world where life makes as much sense as it does from the back of a horse.

Most of all, it is amazing how many lessons about life and about God come from the barn.

After all, true love was born in a barn.

WANT FREE BOOKS?

From time to time Kayla gives away free copies of her new releases. But her promotions are highly temporary! If you would like to be notified when she is giving her kindle books away for free sign up at the following link.

The Rushed Ride

I remember taking one of my horses out for a pleasure ride a couple of years ago. It was a beautiful evening, the sun was setting, the birds were singing and a gentle breeze was turning a hot day into a cool evening.

 Unfortunately, my mare didn't share my sentiment, she'd been relaxing in the pasture and I'd taken her out and made her work! I guess she decided to get this over with as quickly as possible. Her way of thinking was to get from point A to point B and then she could go back home to the pasture and enjoy herself.

Of course, the fastest way to do that was to run. So run she did! She spent the majority of the ride in a very fast and uncomfortable trot. So uncomfortable that it was almost impossible to ride. To fix that, every time she broke into a trot I would turn her in a small circle. Over and over she would break into a run to go home faster, and over and over again I would turn her in a small circle and go back to the starting point.

The ride wound up taking way longer than I had ever planned because she was trying to get home so quickly. The irony of it all struck me. In her eagerness to get the ride over with my mare was actually making it take much longer, plus it was far less pleasant.

I realized that this is similar to what we so often do with God. We're in a rush and he isn't. We want to get this over with and go home, and he doesn't. We need another job, now! But God is taking his time. Every time we try to speed events in

9

our life up and get ahead of Him, He stops us and turns us in a small circle. He hits the rewind button on our lives, so to speak. And in the end, we too, make it take way more time than He ever intended. So relax, quit rushing and enjoy the present moment just as it is.⏹

HEADSET AND PRESSURE

One of the most important things for a horse to learn in my
opinion is "headset." A well-trained horse will carry their
head perpendicular to the ground. Once a horse has been
taught a proper headset they not only look better but they
are more comfortable to ride and more responsive to
pressure on their bit in an emergency.

Unfortunately, it is also one of the most often overlooked
things by riders and trainers. Probably because teaching a
horse correct headset takes a lot of patience and skill.

After my horse learns to respond to pressure on the bit by
bringing their nose in, then I proceed to "Ask for their nose."
When the horse gives me their head I immediately release
the pressure and praise them. After a lot of practice, the
horse will simply carry their nose tucked in without any
pressure.

Recently, one of the horses I was training was having a hard
time just giving me her nose. I remember riding around the
pen and thinking, "If you'd just give me your head, I'd give it
right back to you. And it would be so much more
comfortable for both of us! "

Then a parallel hit me. That's what God does with us. He
says, "If you'd just give Me your life, I'd give it right back to
you only better than you had it before, better for both of us!"

And like that mare maybe we don't think that it will be
comfortable. It doesn't sound like fun, or the thought just
scares us. If we give our life over to God, what exactly will He

ask us to do? Be missionaries in the jungle eating monkey meat and wearing grass skirts?

The Bible talks about this in Matthew 6:31, "So don't worry about these things saying what will we eat? What will we drink? What will we wear? [32] These things dominate the thoughts of unbelievers, but your heavenly Father already knows all your needs.[33] Seek the Kingdom of God above all else, and live righteously, and He will give you everything you need."

Just like a horse who eventually learns how to respond to pressure, we learn to give our lives to God and relax. Are you ready to give?

THE SCARY HORSE EATING MACHINE

When I was a teenager my riding hobby doubled as a side income. I would purchase untrained horses, train them and resell them. I still marvel that I'm alive after some of the stupid stunts I pulled with those horses. My guardian angels must have been exhausted by the end of every summer. But those summers proved to be some of the best summers of my life!

To me, there was nothing more exciting than buying a new horse. I loved wandering through complete stranger's barns and pastures, petting the velvety noses, scratching behind ears and daydreaming about how I could coach any of these horses to win at least five national championships. (Spoiler alert: none of them ever did. Although I do have an alumni barrel horse out there that won a few saddles.) While other girls my age daydreamed about boys and went shopping for clothes every spring, I dreamed of horses and shopped for bloodlines!

One year I had just picked out my next prospect. A beautiful black Arabian gelding, he was gorgeous, had an impressive pedigree, and most importantly in my teenage mind, he had a long mane and tail. Excitedly I helped my father hook up the stock trailer and embarked on the task of bringing him home.

Our yard was perfect for horses. We had a beautiful, luscious forty-acre pasture. It boasted five ponds, beautiful shady oak trees, and in three generations no one in our family had ever grazed it down. To me this pasture was magical, there was nothing more relaxing than a long walk in in the pasture when the sun was setting and the leaves were turning gold. The smell of autumn, the leaves crunching beneath my feet, and a herd of six horses following me wherever I went begging for treats. My horses loved their home too, every spring when they were turned loose in the pasture they would run, buck, rear, and whinny at the sheer joy of their new freedom.

Sadly our horse trailer was not anything like our pasture. Far from being magical, or even scenic, it can only be described a decrepit. It was thirty years old, primarily rust-colored and quite frankly, a rolling junkyard. Although it was sturdy enough to be safe, it most certainly was not pretty. To a horse who had never been in any trailers before, this certainly did not look like a comfortable, happy, or even safe place. Suffice to say, it took three people an hour, a bucket of grain and a lot of coaxing to get my new acquisition into our rust bucket trailer.

To my new horse that trailer was the ultimate destination. He couldn't see past all of the metal and rust to our pasture. He was not thinking about 40 acres of luscious green grass, shady oak trees, or pleasant ponds. All he saw was a cold, rusty, metal horse-eating machine.

In a way, it reminds me of how we humans view death. Psalm 23 speaks of "walking through the valley of the shadow of death." Did you catch that? It's just a shadow!

Like our stock trailer, death appears to be a cold, ugly, and dark place. But in reality, it is just a means of moving from one place to another. Death is not the final destination and we have an advantage over that horse, he didn't know where he was going, he had no way of knowing what lay before him, but we can. God has promised us greener pastures filled with things more beautiful than we could ever imagine. He's never lied to us yet, so why are you afraid of the trailer?

MEETING OSCAR

As long as I can remember I've been enthralled with the idea of jumping horses. There's something magical about the way a horse can jump such incredible heights while balancing a rider on their back. To me, it was the equivalent of sprouting wings.

Then one day I saw an ad for the perfect horse. "Oscar" was so well-trained he had even been used for lessons and was jumping fences as high as four feet. Not a spectacular height, but double what any of my current horses had jumped. Best of all he was cheap! Excitedly I counted my money and we once again hooked up our trailer to take a look.

Oscar was perfect in every way. He had obviously been trained by someone who knew what they were doing. He worked well off of leg pressure and had lovely collected gaits. There was only one problem, and it was a big one. Oscar had what horse people refer to as a "Hard mouth."

You see a horse's mouth is extremely sensitive, and whatever pressure you exert on the reins the horse will feel times three in their mouth.

It's a pretty important mechanism because sometimes if a horse gets spooked and runs away in fear, the reins are your lifelines and tripling the pressure on them becomes important.

The problem when inexperienced riders are put on horses is they are careless with their hands and yank on the reins. That deadens the nerves in the horse's mouth and pretty soon they hardly even feel pressure on the bit. And if the horse ignores the bit he's almost impossible to control. Often it means that you can't stop, turn, or back your horse up. In essence, the horse is ruined.

In Oscar's case, a well-trained, beautiful, registered horse had become virtually unable to be ridden because his nerves in his mouth where deadened.

Often it's the same with people, we don't develop hard mouths though, we develop a hard conscience. We tell ourselves that it's okay to skip reading our bible just this once and ignore the feeling of guilt. We don't go to church on Sunday because we don't feel like it, or we treat someone in an unloving manner while promising ourselves that "we will do better next time."

God pulls on our reins by gently tugging at our conscience and we ignore it. Pretty soon our conscience gets harder and harder until we don't feel anything or the only thing that we can feel is very sharp jabs.

There is nothing more pleasurable that riding a horse that works lightly off of the reins and your legs. Sometimes all you have to do is pick the reins up and the horse will stop before you even make contact with their mouth. That should be our goal with God. To be so in tune with Him that He just has to whisper quietly to our conscience and we skid to whoa.

Oh, Oscar eventually found a loving home with one of my friends. She purchased him as a companion horse and discovered that when she used a bit-less bridle he was quite

17

rideable. He lived the rest of his life out in well-deserved rest.⏹

HOT HORSE SHOES

Recently I attended a horseshoeing school where I got to watch other students practice the art of creating horseshoes. Skilled blacksmiths could make a shoe from a plain metal rod in fifteen minutes. In fact, one blacksmith actually made two horseshoes in about twenty minutes.

I had a chance to fully appreciate exactly how impressive this was when I attempted to make my own horseshoe. Let's just say that I'm much better at observing than creating! If that shoe had been put on a horse, the horse would have come up lame pretty fast!

After we had made the basic shoe shape we would rasp the rough edges off of the shoe. Because I had my shoe heated up so much, the act of rasping easily bent my shoe out of shape.

I couldn't help but think back to the times in my life when God had made the events in my life uncomfortable. I felt I had been placed in a proverbial fire. As the old saying goes, "God whispers to us in the good times and shouts to us in the bad."

Looking back at those "fiery" times in my life I can see how God was using the heat to bend me and shape me. Once we have been heated up, God knows that just a small amount of pressure will bend us and influence us. So if you are going through a hard time, stop and ask God what it is that He's trying to show you. Then, listen close, because even if God is shouting, we still have to listen.

BEYOND BASICS

A coworker and I were discussing . . . you guessed it, horses. He was considering buying a horse from a particular trainer and asked for my opinion. I told him that the trainer's horses were okay, but all those horses did were go forward, backward, and turn right or left.

He mulled this over for a minute and then asked me quizzically, "What else should they do?"

Good question, what else is there for a horse to do? At first, at a glance, it seems like that is all that there is to do. But if only people understood that there is so much more! A horse should bend around your leg, collect their hindquarters underneath you, travel straight sideways when asked. You should be able to increase and decrease the speed of their gait. They should bend their head around to your knee in a relaxed manner when asked. The list goes on and on.

In fact, I've never owned a horse yet who I've run out of things to teach. Horses can continue to learn their whole life. However, many people are content with the basics. All they want to do is go forward, backward, and turn right or left.

I have always thought that if these people only knew what they were missing, that they would never again be happy with just that. Being able to go forward, backward, right and left is just the beginning.

Much like being a Christian. Believing is just the beginning! 2 Peter 1:5 says " . . . Supplement your faith with a generous provision of moral excellence, and moral excellence with knowledge, [6] and knowledge with self-control, and self-control with patient endurance, and patient endurance with godliness, [7] and godliness with brotherly affection, and brotherly affection with love for everyone." All of the amazing things that we can learn! It's a list that I defy any Christian to master.

The sad part is that many Christians, just like many horse owners, are content with just believing, just the basics. Who needs all of the extras? If they only knew what they were missing, they would never be content with so little. The sad part is that as a Christian, being content with so little has much larger ramifications.

?

THE SCARY BLUE TARP

Horses are naturally afraid of man. Though it may not be what you see in the 'Black Stallion', or 'My Friend Flicka', in nature horses are wild animals whose best defense is to run away. Getting a horse quiet enough to accept a bit and saddle calmly takes a lot of work, time, and trust.

A major part of this training is "desensitizing" the horse. There are many ways of doing this. A common one is to take an object that horses are usually afraid of, such as a plastic tarp, place the horse in a small pen, and shake the tarp around them until the horse is no longer afraid. Eventually, the horse will become comfortable enough to actually walk over the plastic tarp.

You would think that after having completed this exercise that the horse would now only be unafraid of plastic tarps. But other loud, bright-colored or fast-moving objects would still scare him.

That's true, and it's not true. The tarp exercise teaches a horse much more than simply that bright-colored crackly tarps don't eat horses for breakfast! It also teaches them to trust their handlers. A horse catches on very fast that humans are "safe places." After they learn to trust you, they will go almost anywhere for you. They'll walk over and through other scary objects without panicking, just because you asked them to.

I often think of how this aspect of horse training reflects what God sometimes does with us. Sometimes God has to scare us good. Sometimes it takes a big blow to the head, like a scary diagnosis, or the loss of a loved one.

Whatever your personal crisis is, God will take you through it. Once it's over you'll turn around, look back and realize that during that desensitizing process, He was right there for you. He was your safe place, and your trust level in Him will go way up. After that, even you will be surprised at just what you will go through and around, just because He asked you to.

⁉

THAT TIME I MADE A MISTAKE

It's no secret, I make mistakes. A lot of them, sometimes very stupid ones! Just ask someone who knows me. They'll probably be able to produce a long list of them. (On second thought maybe don't ask...)

On one particular occasion, I took my mare to an all-day riding event. In anticipation of the big day I bathed her, combed her mane and tail and put her in a box stall overnight. That way all I had to do the next morning was load her up and take off for the day.

When we took a break for lunch I happened to ride by a water trough and noticed my mare pulling towards it. To my horror, I realized that I hadn't offered my poor mare water since the night before! I felt so guilty, how could I forget something as basic to a horse as water?

Thank God that He doesn't make mistakes like that! The bible tells us that God is the Good Shepherd. In the famous Psalm 23, we are told that "He leads us beside the still waters." And you can rest assured that He won't forget!

I'm so thankful that someone who is far more competent than me is in charge of my life. He's perfect, blameless, and wants only the best for us. He's not going to forget about us, screw up our lives (even by accident) or make any mistakes. We are safe, protected and well-handled in His care. What an awesome God!

Now excuse me I have to go suck up to my mare.

MIND READING 101

Once you've ridden a horse, for even a small amount of time, you and the horse develop an amazing rhythm. One of the things I love about horses is how the two of us seem to share the same mind.

Many, many times I've been riding a horse and all I had to do was think about changing gaits just to have my horse voluntarily do it before I even asked.

This happens because when a rider thinks about trotting, they subconsciously tense their muscles and lean forward ever so slightly. Horses are amazingly sensitive to even the smallest movement and will anticipate your commands.

Likewise, I can feel when my horse is about to break into a trot. They bring their nose in slightly and tuck their hindquarters underneath them in preparation.

Not long ago I was riding a young horse for one of the first times. He was understandably tense and nervous and kept trying to break into a trot. I repeatedly turned him in small circles to slow him down and get his mind off of running for his life.

He was trying to behave, but he was nervous, and the temptation was so great! As a rider, I could physically feel the battle going on inside of him over whether he should run for his life or just stay calm. I could also feel myself rooting for him to stay calm and was doing my best to talk him down and help him work through everything.

25

I wonder, how does God feel when He can see us considering whether or not to disobey? Surely if I could tell that my horse was tempted, God can tell when we are being tempted. I wonder, does He watch and hope that we won't? Does He cheer when we don't? Does He try and find a way to get our mind off of it? Or try to warn us of the consequences? I wonder if He whispers in our ear the way I do to my horse?

The bible tells us that Jesus is praying for us. (Romans 8:34) What an incredible thought! Think about it next time you're facing temptation, Jesus is praying for *you*!

THE SPOILED MARE

The horse I am currently training has been the easiest one yet. His worst misbehavior to date has been a mild spook. He hasn't bucked, reared, balked, or anything "wrong" yet. I think there is a two-fold reason for how easy this has been. The first reason is quite simple, he is a horse with a calm and willing disposition. The second reason is that this is a horse I have owned since the day he was born. I've trained him to behave exactly how I want him to right from day one.

At the same time as I have been breaking this horse, I've been riding a horse that belongs to a friend. My friend's horse has a different history. She had some proper training when she was young, but was then sold to a family with small children who knew very little about how to properly handle a horse. She very quickly got the better of them and became spoiled.

She is not by any means an unrideable mare, in fact, she can be quite an enjoyable ride when she's in the right mood. But she can also be extremely frustrating! Sometimes she is so balky that we have to fight for upwards of fifteen minutes just to walk across the yard.

It serves to prove that a green(*young or untrained*) horse is preferable to a spoiled horse. Sometimes it's better if a horse knows nothing than if they know all of the wrong things.

I've often found this to be true with "religious people." They are basically good people. They aren't alcoholics, cocaine addicts, or murderers, so they, therefore, can consider themselves to be "Christians" even though they really understand very little about God. Some of them attend

27

church every week, some are quite sincere and devout in their beliefs. They don't understand that being a Christian is about what you are doing, instead of about what you are not doing.

You aren't a follower of Christ just because you have never murdered anyone or did drugs. You are a true believer when you admit that you are a sinner, accept Christ's forgiveness for what you have done, and choose to follow him with all of your heart. Many "good" people find this concept hard to grasp.

It's hard for anybody to admit to being wrong, especially people who are basically good and have sterling reputations. These people attend church every Sunday, they know all the songs, they've possibly even been baptized and they think that they are Christians because of it.

Paul talks about these people in 2 Timothy 3:5, he said that they "Have a form of Godliness, but denying its power."

These people are somewhat similar to a spoiled horse, who has learned just enough to appear like Christians outwardly while never doing what is asked of them.

They are much more difficult than a person who knows nothing and will admit to you that they know nothing. So please, if you are "religious," or "Christian" or even a "good person" ask yourself, why? What made you that way? When did you become that? Is it really true?

Why Do We Need A Dog?

We have a black lab/collie cross dog named Keeta. In the past, we have owned dogs for various reasons. Some were purebred dogs that we used to breed; others helped to chase the cattle or alerted us to trespassers.

Keeta doesn't do any of that. She is our most useless dog to date. She's not registered, or even purebred for that matter, there is really no point in breeding her. She tries to help chase the cattle, but she's afraid of them, and when she does get up the nerve to help, she almost always chases them in the wrong direction. She has never even figured out that she's supposed to bark at cars when they come onto the yard.

In fact, her most useful trait is that she's relatively large and black. So the very odd person who is afraid of a big black dog (with a wagging tail) is intimidated into staying in their vehicle.

The other day as I was petting her I began to wonder why we keep such a useless animal on the farm. She is the only animal we own that does absolutely nothing to earn her keep. But really it's not much of a mystery, we keep her for companionship. No one on earth is ever as happy to see me as Keeta is. Even if I'm only gone for ten minutes I get the biggest and best "welcome home" that she can muster. She is content to follow me around outside for hours on end just for the privilege of being near me.

It very much reminds me of the age-old question, "Why does God need man?" After all, what does man do for God that God cannot do for himself? What can man give to God that God does not already have? Isn't everything God's to begin with?

The answer is very much like the reason that we keep Keeta, we are here to be companions to God. To worship, obey, and have fellowship with the King of Kings. God does not "need" us, any more that we need Keeta.

Often we like to imagine that God would be lost without us or that we are somehow indispensable to His great plan. We get so caught up in the importance of all the things we are doing for God, that we miss the main point. We are here primarily for fellowship with Him. Every other activity we have is secondary to that, so the question is, are you doing your job?

Harnessing A Temper Tantrum

We had some family friends who were looking for an affordable pony for their children. Since a good kid's pony is about as rare as a yellow diamond we suggested the option of buying a young pony and training it to ride and drive with our assistance.

That is how we came home with Dancer. He turned out to be quite a handful. To put it in a nutshell, he was mean, vicious, snotty, and stubborn. We suspected that at some point in his life he may have been abused, it was pretty much the only logical explanation for his behavior.

The first time we attempted to put somebody on Dancer's back he sent them up in an impressive arc before they hit the ground. After literally months of round pen work and ground driving, we decided to attempt to hook Dancer up to our pony cart.

Carefully we attached Dancer's harness to the cart. We put someone on either side of him or a third person walking behind the pony cart driving. That way if Dancer panicked and ran when he felt the weight of the cart behind him no one would have to jump out. It turned out to be a wise choice because when Dancer realized that the cart was attached to him he reacted violently.

He ran, kicked, bucked, you name it, he did it. Most horses will carry on for a few minutes, then realize the cart isn't going to hurt them and relax. But Dancer kept it up for at least an hour.

The funny thing is the cart that we hooked him to was actually quite light. It was made specifically for breaking horses to pull and actually is only slightly harder to pull than a bicycle.

Jan 5, 2020

In Matthew 11:30 Jesus said, "For my yoke is easy and my burden is light." This verse often makes me think of Dancer. Like him sometimes, I kick, squeal and throw a fuss when God asks me to do something. Even if it's something very small. I'm not always sure if it's fear, anger, or both that cause me to behave like that. But when I'm in the middle of my temper tantrum, God whispers to me "My yoke is easy, and my burden is light." Then I realize just how much worse it really could be.

I'm angry and fussing over something that in the grand scheme of things is actually light and easy to pull, just like that cart.

⁈

THE SPECIAL HORSE

I currently have a herd of ten horses. They are all at varying stages in their growth and training. But if I was to go out into that pen today, only one of those horses would call to me and come running over to greet me. Only one would try to herd the other horses away so he could have me all to himself, and only one would beg for treats.

From the time I knew for sure that his mother was pregnant I knew Ringo was going to be special. I absolutely adored his mother and hoped beyond hope that he would turn out to be something like her. I also allowed a tiny part of me to hope that she would have a colt instead of a filly, i.e. a male instead of a female. And an even smaller part of me hoped that he would be roan-colored like his stud (or father) was.

I knew my chances of getting one or all of those things were pretty slim, after all, you can't special order babies. I knew that I would love him no matter how he acted or what color he was.

Imagine my delight when the foal turned out to be a gorgeous roan colt with all of the fire and personality that his mother had displayed. I loved him from the moment I first saw him and played with him every chance I got. It took all of my patience to wait until he was old enough to start riding. When he was finally old enough to train I was amazed at how compliant he was.

It only took twenty rides for him to start acting like an old trail horse. Most of my horses took more like forty or fifty rides. To this day he has never offered a serious

33

misbehavior, not one buck, rear, kick, nothing. The beautiful part is that the more I ride him the more eager he is to be caught.

One day I was sitting on a hay bale and watching him eat grass in the pasture, trying to figure out what exactly I had done right with this horse. I wanted to repeat it with my other horses!

Was it all of the groundwork? Maybe sneaking him sugar? What was it that made him so eager to please and so relaxed around me? I realized that this horse knows he is special to me. It was everything I did with him. All of the time I spent petting him, talking to him, all of it. He knows that I adore him, and he adores me in return. He loves me and wants to make me happy, no matter what it takes. He'll do whatever I tell him, and he'll do it happily.

Jan 5.2020

In 1 John 5:3, the bible says, "For this is the love of God, that we keep his commandments: and his commandments are not grievous." Not just that we do what He says, but that we do it happily. Not a begrudging, 'if I have to' obedience, but one that is willing and excited to be doing God's work. Just like that Ringo, easy to catch and eager to please.

⍰

34

EVERY KNEE WILL BOW

I have always wanted to learn how to teach a horse tricks. I have witnessed others teach their horses to fetch, count, pick up pens, nod their heads, rear and even balance on a seesaw.

These tricks are an amazing tribute to a horse's natural athleticism and intelligence. Many of these tricks go against a horse's natural instinct.

For instance, a horse will rarely lie down unless they are completely relaxed and convinced of their safety. A horse's main defense against a predator is running and when they lie down or bow, they are making themselves vulnerable. They will only lie down when a human is near if they have complete trust in that specific human. Yet I have seen trainers get their horses to lie down or bow in front of about two hundred strange humans.

Unfortunately, my own attempts at getting my mare to bow were met with a great deal more resistance and an alarmed look from my horse that shouted: "What in the world are you trying to make me do now?" Spoiler alert: I have never mastered this trick.

It brought to mind Phil 2:10 "That at the name of Jesus every knee should bow, of things in heaven, and things in earth, and things under the earth." It's a bit startling when you really start to think about it. The bible doesn't just say every man will bow, it says everything will bow. Even my horses, even my dog, everything!

Things under the earth, can you imagine, all of the bugs, wild animals, pets, your neighbor, everybody and everything. Wow! So even if I can't show my mare just exactly how to bow at the present, I won't have to worry, because someday she will do it with ease.

[?]

REINS

Reins are pretty important things. (Reins are what you hold in your hands when riding a horse). They are kind of like the steering wheel on your horse. If you drop your reins you risk losing control of your horse.

There are an amazing variety of reins available, leather, nylon, rubber, etc. Some have silver decals or pretty bangles. Some of them attach to the horse's bridle with a screw, and some just clip on. You can buy split reins or roping reins that are attached to each other so you can't drop them. Some reins have leather "poppers" on the back that you can use them to make noises that will encourage a young horse to move during their first rides.

Personally, I like to ride with a set of thick braided reins; they won't break easily, and also won't cut into my hands. I prefer if these reins are split and have a popper on the end. It may seem like these are a fairly insignificant piece of equipment, but they should not be underestimated, your life can depend on how strong they are. I have had a set of reins break in the middle of a bucking fit and the results were terrifying and quite painful.

Imagine my surprise when reading through the Old Testament and finding multiple references to reins. Only these reins don't' go to a horse's bit, they go to my heart.

In Jeremiah 17:10 God said, "I the Lord search the heart, I try the reins, even to give every man according to his ways, and according to the fruit of his doing."

There is an exercise I do with every horse when I start riding them. I teach them to bring their nose right around to touch my toe when I pull on the rein. I do that exercise hundreds of times until the horse will respond to just the slightest pressure.

It is an extremely important exercise because when a horse is bucking, running away, or even rearing, pulling their nose around to your stirrup stops it. As long as the horse has their head in that position their spine is bent, making it impossible to buck or rear, and they can only run in a tight little circle.

However, no matter how responsive my horse is to bit-pressure, it won't do me any good if my reins break. For that reason, I regularly inspect my reins to ensure my safety.

Sometimes I wonder, am I as careful with the "reins of my heart" as I am with the reins of my horse? Those reins are far more valuable and important than any leather reins I will ever purchase!

⁇

The "Horse Eating" Oak

I have a little mare right now that I've just started riding. She has been ridden about twelve times, all of these rides have taken place in an enclosed arena. An arena can get boring for a horse and rider pretty fast. I mean seriously, you can only do so many laps and figure eights before a young horse, much like a young child will become bored.

It's best to take the horse out of the riding ring and on a long relaxing trail ride as soon as possible. Although when the horse only has twelve rides so far, a trail ride can get pretty scary for them.

Such was the case with Cheyenne. We only got about forty feet away from the barn when Cheyenne balked. I gave her a little nudge with my legs to tell her it was alright and she turned and ran as fast as she could back to the barn. She was just too scared to keep going.

The reason she couldn't continue? An unusually large oak tree which was situated too close to the road for her comfort. It seemed that the more I clucked to her, bumped her with my legs and put pressure on her, the more stubborn she became. It was simply too much to ask of her to walk past the "horse eating" oak tree.

Suddenly it struck me how this must have felt from her perspective. Cheyenne was a sweet little filly, rarely balky, always eager to please and she had always placed a lot of trust in me. If walked through something scary she would happily follow.

In her mind, I'm always there to help. But now here she was facing this big scary object, and instead of helping her I'm sitting up there making noise and kicking her.

I could just feel this little filly underneath me screaming "Help! This tree is going to kill me!" I could also feel her frustration, from her perspective she was not getting help from me. In fact, I was making things worse.

Just like so many times in my life when I've looked up to heaven and cried out "God! Why aren't you helping me?! Where are you? Why are you letting this happen? Can't you see that this situation is going to destroy me?" Only later to realize that He was right there helping me the whole time. Helping me to grow and learn by letting painful things happen to me.

The things I thought would destroy me, would become the very things that would create me. In Hebrews 13:5 God said, "I will never leave you or forsake you." It may not always feel like it, but He is there with us, and believe it or not He is helping us.

▢

WHERE IS YOUR MIND AT?

I've been around horses since I was born. As a little girl, every spare minute was spent in the barn with the horses. Now that I am an adult every spare minute is spent in the barn with the horses.

Some things don't change much. Yet despite all the time I've spent with, watching and learning about horses, I have so much to learn about them.

That is why I found myself curled up with a horse magazine one rainy afternoon, reading an article on loading horses into trailers.

Many horses are afraid of the dark, confined interior of a trailer. Some horses have had bad experiences in a trailer and simply don't want to repeat them. Either way, many horses are quite hard to load.

The article pointed out that a horse's mind is usually wherever the horse is looking. For instance, if you are riding your horse, and he has his ears and eyes pointed to the left, it is safe to assume that his mind is in that direction as well.

A lot of handlers wait until the horse points his ears into the trailer, meaning that they have their mind in the trailer, and then they tend to swat the horse in order to encourage them to get in. Talk about confusing the poor animal, it was just beginning to think about getting in and then it gets punished. I guess he won't think about that again!

I found this article of particular interest because in some ways it is possible to read a horse's mind. Once you have spent enough time around a horse, you get in tune with them, and you have a pretty good idea what they are going to do next. I guess it's kind of like intuition, I think it is one of the most awesome benefits of being with horses.

Yet it is only a vague shadow of how well God knows our minds. He always knows what I'm going to do before I do it. He knows things about my mind that I don't even know because He created it.

Not only that, He is able to take thoughts out, and put new thoughts in. He doesn't have to wait until He sees my eyes go a particular direction; He doesn't study my body language and wonder what is going on in my mind. He knows, beyond a shadow of a doubt what I'm going to do, and why I am going to do it. I can't keep secrets from Him; there are no safes that we can stash our secret thoughts in where He can't see them. He also tells us that, "As a man thinks in his heart so is He." Think about it, what are you trying to hide from God?

⍰

HORSES AND HOBBIES

Do you have a hobby? Maybe it's a sport you love, like golf. Maybe you like to paint, sew, or work on cars. Perhaps you are like me and you enjoy writing. Usually, a person's hobby is their passion. They work 9-5 because they have to, then they come home and work twice as hard on their hobby and love every minute of it. A hobby is usually something that you find to be fun, relaxing, inspiring, or enjoyable.

I personally have several hobbies, but probably the one that takes up the bulk of my free time is my horses. I love to train, ride, groom, and just play with them. I don't begrudge them even one second of my time. I happily spend my spare change on tack, equipment, feed, and shots. I eagerly look forward to having time to spend with them.

Recently somebody challenged me, they asked me what the most important thing in my life is. Now if you are a Christian you should be able to join with me in saying that it is your faith. Then this person asked me what would happen if I put as much time, money and energy into my faith as I did into my hobby.

Whoa! What a radical thought, I would be spending entire afternoons studying my Bible and praying, I would invest hundreds of dollars in Bible commentaries, concordances, books, and devotionals.

I'm embarrassed to admit that I currently own more books about horses than about Christianity. Even more telling is the fact that I have to confess to having read the collection of horse-related books much closer and much more frequently than my faith-based books.

If the Bible was my hobby, I would be spending my weekends in it, not the barn. Instead of going on weekend trail rides, I would go to weekend faith retreats.

I would have spent more time watching church services on TV, and less time watching professional horse trainers telling me how to get a perfectly collected trot from my horse.

Now this is a pretty radical lifestyle. Surely it's too much to ask us to take our faith that far . . . right? Or is it?

I may say that my faith is the most important thing in my life, but when it comes right down to it, can I back that up with my actions? This person left me with the same challenge I am going to leave you with, to make the Bible your hobby.

Not just any hobby, but your primary hobby. Invest in it, your time, money, and energy. After all, God invested in you.

[?]

HE WON'T BUCK

A friend of mine has been a horse trainer for more than ten years. After spending that long in any business you are bound to have a few interesting stories to tell, and he certainly is no exception!

One story he tells really stuck with me. He says it happens to him all of the time. People buy colts and do groundwork on them, but are afraid to get on for the first ride. So they call him.

When they bring the animal to him, they explain that all of the groundwork is done, and they are one hundred percent sure that the horse won't buck, but they are just too timid to climb on.

At this point, my friend will take the horse, and begin doing some simple groundwork exercises. He relates that almost always the owners will act confused, "What are you doing?" they ask, "I did all those things already. He's not going to buck; you just have to get on."

"You're sure he's not going to buck?" He'll ask. Invariably the response is a firm "Yes." "Really sure about that?" He asks again, with a twinkle in his eye.

At that point, my friend hands the reins back to the owner and says, "Okay, then you get on." The owner always backpedals as fast as possible and sputters, "Well, I can't do that . . . he might buck!"

Let me ask you a question, do these owners really believe that their horses won't buck? The truth is no matter how much you claim to believe something, or how certain you think you are about it, you only believe it as much as you are willing to back it up with your actions.

Put another way, you may say you are a Christian, you may say that you believe that God will provide for all of your needs. But when you get laid off from work do you worry and fret? Do you really believe that God will provide for all of your needs? Or somewhere deep down inside of you, do you think that there is a slight chance that the horse might buck?

But wait! I have good news for you, horses are moody and unpredictable. They change from day to day, so no matter how much groundwork I have done with my horse, there is always a slight chance that the horse might spook at something and buck.

Jan 6. 2020

But our God is the same yesterday, today, and forever. He's not going to change, there's not even a slight chance that He's going have a glitch or change his mind. I would rather have faith in God than in my horse any day! So go ahead, trust God and don't be afraid to back your words up with actions.

THE SAFE SPOT

Being a third generation horse fanatic, it surprised me to learn that the methods used to break a horse have changed drastically since my grandparent's days.

Since horses have been employed by mankind for centuries, one would have thought that various training methods would have been exhausted about a thousand years ago. I have often wondered why it didn't happen that way, but it seems that every ten to fifteen years someone comes up with a groundbreaking new approach to horses.

In recent years a common method of training horses has been to "round pen" them. The basic theory is to simulate a horse's natural environment; the trainer stands in the middle of a round pen and "herds" the horse in a circle around themselves. One of the first things the horse learns is that when they are in the middle of the pen beside the trainer they get to rest. But as soon as they leave the trainer's side they have to work harder. The lesson is that life is easy as long as the horse is near the trainer, but if he tries to run away, he just makes it harder for himself. This method helps horses bond with humans as it closely simulates how horses behave in their herds.

Recently I brought home a young mare who was by far the easiest round pen prospect I have ever worked with. It only took her about five minutes to figure out what I wanted. Whenever something would scare her she would whirl around, run straight towards me and bury her face in my

47

chest. I could almost hear her saying "Help! I'm scared! You're the only safe place I know!"

In a similar fashion, whenever my life is going wrong, or something is scaring me, I too, should know enough to whirl around and run straight for God. He is indeed the only truly safe place I know. Just like the round pen, when I was running away from and trying to distance myself from God, I just made life harder for myself. But when I run towards him and beg for help, He always comes through for me.

⁇

HELMET HAIR

Did you know that your brain is the texture of not-quite-set jelly? I came across this interesting tidbit of information during a helmet awareness campaign which was run by our local 4-H club. However, despite being subjected to some very convincing information concerning helmet safety, I refused to wear a helmet for fear of looking like a "sissy."

You see, I ride "western" meaning my saddle looks like a cowboy's, and my hat, if I wore any at all, was a cowboy hat. Only "sissy" people who ride "English" and wear tight pants wore helmets!

My opinion on helmets remained unchanged throughout my teen years. I would usually wear protective gear for a horse's first ride, but as soon as I was satisfied that this particular horse wasn't going to buck, my helmet would return to its shelf to collect a new layer of dust.

Then when I was about seventeen I decided to learn to ride English. Now to their credit English riders don't seem to be as obsessed about appearing "sissy". You will rarely find a properly attired English rider that does not have a helmet on their head.

One afternoon I was out riding English. Thankfully there happened to be a photographer there that day, so I thought in order to appear like a proper English rider I would don my helmet for only the second time that year and only because I thought it would look good. It's amazing how God looks out for me despite my vain stupidity!

I warmed my horse up and then approached a small training jump. Since I had only jumped my horse about three times prior to this, my seat over the jump was very poor.

My horse did not like to jump naturally, so in protest, he ran up to the jump, lifted his front feet off the ground . . . and changed his mind. He slammed down on top of the jump, and unseated me in a very un-photogenic manner!

I did manage to go over the jump, just not with my horse. I landed head first on the ground about 3 feet in front of the fence. The force of my body weight coming down on my helmet cracked it right open. Boy, was I ever grateful that I had chosen to look "sissy" that day!

Despite the "splitting" headache (please pardon the pun) I managed to take in all of the facts and realized that had I been in my normal riding attire, I would at very least have a concussion now, and at worst be dead. I learned my lesson that day, and now I almost always wear a helmet when riding. I have been accused of looking sissy and I really don't care anymore. I prefer to be alive!

The Bible also talks about an important helmet, the helmet of salvation in Ephesians 6:17 "Put on salvation as your helmet, and take the sword of the Spirit, which is the word of God."

A helmet is the most basic layer of protective gear for any discipline, are you wearing yours?

⏀

READING MY HORSE'S MIND

Sometimes training a horse can involve an aspect of detective work. If a horse is acting out it can be tricky to figure out the exact reason why.

Recently I was out riding my mare and she unexpectedly began to buck. I got her stopped but for the life of me I couldn't figure out why she had ever started.

This mare was usually quiet and super dependable, in fact, I'd even let some of my little nieces and nephews ride her. I spent the rest of my ride on her trying to figure out what would have caused such behavior and decided that I would probably never know exactly what had set her off.

Then I took her saddle off, I realized that my new girth had been rubbing her wrong, and she had a girth gall. *(A girth gall is horseman's term for a blister caused by an ill-fitting girth).* No wonder the poor thing had bucked!

At times I am amazed at how seamlessly my horse can communicate with me. And yet at other times the language barrier between me and my horse can seem overwhelming.

I love that God can always communicate to us exactly what He needs us to know. I love that there is never a communication barrier between God and myself like there sometimes is between my horse and me.

God never has to wonder why I did what I did, and unlike my horse, I never have to wonder what in the world it is that God wants from me this time. I can be confident in the knowledge that He will let me know at the right time.

THE STUPID HORSE

At a recent horse clinic, a rider was having a very difficult time with her horse. As the day went on the horse's list of misdemeanors grew longer and longer. The rider became increasingly frustrated and near the end of the day she glared at the horse and muttered under her breath "stupid horse!"

The clinician looked up at her and said, "Do you really think that this horse is stupid?" Embarrassed to have been overheard, the rider hemmed and hawed for a couple seconds before admitting that she did indeed think her horse was stupid.

 The clinician allowed a slow easy-going smile to spread across his face, and then with a twinkle in his eye he said, "Good than you should have no problems outsmarting your stupid horse."

I have since then come to appreciate the value of a stupid horse. When you think about what horses allow us to do with them, they really are quite stupid sometimes.

I probably weigh less than one tenth of my horse's weight. I'm not nearly as strong as him, and I certainly lack the ability to run as fast and as long as he can. He can bite harder, kick harder, and pull harder and that is all *before* I get on his back, which by the way he doesn't have to allow either.

Yet I can make my horse do almost anything I want. I can put a rope around his neck and lead him wherever I want, pass things that scare him, and take him through obstacles that he certainly doesn't like. It never crosses his mind to pull back and run away, because when he was a baby I could out-pull him.

In fact, one of the most challenging things a horseman can face is a truly smart horse. These horses are the ones that learn how to manipulate their gate handles and get out at night. Smart horses are the ones that will present you with training challenges you've never even heard of before. Smart horses want to know *why* do I have to do that? And can you *make* me do that?

Don't get me wrong, once you have a smart horse trained, they are exceptional at whatever they put their mind to. They make great athletes, famous racehorses, and top-quality bloodlines.

But unless you have an Olympic dream, you should really consider buying a dumb horse. Dumb horses are so much easier to work with. They don't think of creative misbehavior, they don't ask "why?" at every command, and they rarely ever put up a big long fight. They just go with the flow and take whatever comes their way. Be prepared to get some strange looks when you say you are shopping for a dumb horse!

I couldn't help but be reminded of this when I was reading in 1 Corinthians 1:22 "For the Jews seek after a sign, and the Greeks seek after wisdom. [23] But we preach Christ crucified, unto the Jews a stumbling block and unto the Greeks foolishness. Vs. [25] . . . not many wise men after the flesh, not many mighty, and not many noble are called."

Paul is saying that the simplicity of the gospel confounds many scholars and Ph.D.'s. It's so simple that they just can't believe it. So often we think that it has to be harder than this, there must be some good work we have to perform or some amount of money we have to give. Just like a smart horse, they can't seem to quit asking "why?" and begin to believe. It seems foolish to them, and yet it is the most important thing we will ever encounter.

WHAT IS YOUR NUMBER?

My riding pen is surrounded by tall pine trees. They serve to break the wind, provide shade, and in the winter they stop the snow from blowing into the yard.

My mother bought them and her father helped plant them. The story goes my grandfather was about 70 at the time. They started planting in the morning and Mom told me that around noon Grandpa stopped working, leaned on his shovel, heaved a sigh and said, "I guess I won't live to see them grow up." It was a sobering thought, but probably true.

Psalm 90:10 provides a reality check, "Our days may come to seventy years, or eighty, if our strength endures".

My grandfather realized that his chance of living past eighty was pretty slim. The story is memorable to me because of the irony, you see Grandpa is ninety-five years old now, the trees are full grown, and my mother passed away three years ago. A year before she died she was out in the yard with my grandfather and she pointed to the trees, "Remember saying that you wouldn't live to see those grow up?" she asked with a sly smile on her face. He shook his head, "I never thought that I would live this long" he replied.

Death is a part of life, and while I don't believe we should dwell on it constantly, I do believe that it is something to give serious consideration to. Psalm 90 also says, "So teach us to number our days, that we may apply our hearts unto wisdom." How many days are left until you turn eighty? How many weeks? How many summer vacations? How many more gardens will you get to plant? Will you even live to turn eighty?

But most important is why we are supposed to number our days, "So that we may apply our hearts unto wisdom." We're not supposed to worry about whether or not we're going to die or obsess about how long we have left. Rather we are supposed to focus on God and His word, and every once in a while look at those little reminders, the "pine trees" in your life, and remember to number your days.

⁇

The Barrel Pattern

A few months ago I got to watch a popular horse trainer work with a young girl whose horse was out of control. This girl had recently taken up the rodeo sport of running barrels. Barrels are a timed event where the horse runs a specific pattern around 3 barrels and the person with the fastest time wins.

Imagine this from the horse's perspective, you run the same pattern the same way all the time, it never ever changes. Not surprisingly these horses often get out of control, the rider points the horses at the barrel and the horse quits taking instructions from the rider they just run the pattern the way they know how.

It was really neat to watch the trainer work with this young girl. To remedy the problem he has her set up the barrels in the shape of the pattern, then run her horses up to each individual barrel. BUT, instead of running the pattern the rider was instead supposed to make the horse stop and stand by the barrel.

It was so much fun to watch the confusion on the horse's face and body. But after about half an hour of doing that the horse began to pay attention to the rider instead of assuming that they were always going to do the same thing. After several days of changing the pattern and doing different exercises with the horse, this young girl was able to run a much cleaner and much faster barrel pattern.

It made me think of my life as a Christian and wonder how often I put my life on autopilot. How many times do I simply go through the motions of going to church on Sunday but never stop to actually listen to what God is saying to me?

How often do we as Christians open up our Bibles or sing our worship songs and go through the motions all while planning out our day in the back of our minds? All the while patting ourselves on the back for being "good" Christians and doing the "right" thing. I watched that horse run a beautiful pattern after three days of work, and I vowed to listen to God much closer in the future.　　Jan 7, 2020

Revisiting The Basics

One of the first horses I started with was a pretty little bay mare that I dubbed Hickory. Her training came along so smoothly, it was amazing. (Especially considering how little I knew at the time). It only took a few months before she became an awesome, reliable, and responsive mount. I got the chance to take her on some fun trail rides in a nearby valley, to some clinics with local trainers and had her coming along wonderfully, except . . .

Except that every time I asked her to lope she would toss in about three bucks and then pick up the lope. Her bucks were so tiny that I hardly felt them, but they still concerned me. I was planning on taking her to a local horse show that summer and I knew I would lose some pretty major points with any judge if my horse started bucking in the middle of her pattern.

I asked other horse friends for advice but no one I asked was quite sure what to do. Since the behavior stumped me I finally decided to take her to a local trainer I knew.

When I unloaded her at the trainer's yard and explained the problem I had been having the trainer suggested that I hop on and show her. So I obediently tacked up and climbed aboard. I began by putting my mare through some basic exercises to get her warmed up, walk, trot, halt, back up, all things that she had been doing well and we really had no problems doing.

But the trainer had plenty of advice for us "sit up straighter, drop your heels, quit pulling on the reins so much . . ." The advice went on and on and on. She dished the advice out in a kind way and as I tried it I realized that she was absolutely right.

The strange thing is none of this was new advice to me. I'd been told all of it over and over again and it was all pretty basic stuff. But I desperately needed a reminder about the basics.

Often I think our faith is like that. How many times have we been told that God loves us, that we can trust Him, that we should pray about everything, etc., etc., etc?

These are all things that we know in our heads but sometimes when somebody tells you the same old thing at a different time in your life it means so much more.

For instance, when a Sunday school teacher tells you as a small child that God loves you, it's not so hard to believe. But when you're much older and you've amassed a long list of wrong, it means so much more to have someone put their arm around you and say "God loves you."

My story has a happy ending, the trainer only needed about a week to get my mare to stop bucking at a lope and we were able to go and have fun at the horse show that summer.

But more importantly I learned a lesson, you can never be told the most basic things too often.

⁂

THE HORSE THAT CHANGED MY LIFE

Recently I saw a beautiful poster, it featured some horses grazing in the pasture and scrawled across the picture were the words "that one horse that changed your life." Although I have a long list of horses to choose from, my mind instantly went to TC.

TC came into my life quite by accident. My best friend called up one day and announced that she was going to get a horse, she asked if my mother and I would come horse shopping with them to help them find a suitable mount. We happily agreed and set a date.

That's how I met Tender Care or TC as she was better known. A stunning grey Arab mare with enough getup and go for two people. You never had to touch TC's side to get her going you just had to lift the reins a bit and lean forward. Often it was hard to keep her speed down to a walk.

Not everyone likes a horse like that, but I LOVED her. I climbed on to test drive her and climbed off five minutes later completely in love. I could tell that my mother was in love too, which was awesome because I was only about thirteen at the time.

Before we left I wrapped my arms around her neck to give her a hug only to have her politely pull back and lift her head out of my reach. "TC doesn't hug" her owner informed me.

The problem was you can't go looking at a horse for a friend and then buy it out from under them. So we politely recommended to my friend that she purchase TC, and I was excited for her when she did. (and only a *teeny* bit jealous.)

About a year later my friend's family called again, they had decided that they wanted to sell TC, did we know anyone who would be interested? Why yes we did! The next week they dropped her off at our yard and I got my wish.

She was perfect for me; she tested me at every turn and made me really learn how to ride, while at the same time babysitting me. Even when her behavior was at its worst I always felt safe on her. All through my teen years we went to every horsey thing together, shows, trail rides, 4-H clinics, almost all of my friends rode her and she even had a stunning baby foal for me. Throughout all those years I never did manage to get a proper hug out of her, it turned out her original owner was right. TC did not hug.

I continued to learn more and more about horses, and once I got to be about sixteen I began to break horses. I became more and more absorbed with my "young" horses and one fall I realized that I had only ridden TC twice that year.

We discussed the idea of selling TC, it seemed silly to swallow the cost of feeding and caring for a horse when I only rode her twice a year. But as you can imagine the idea of selling my girl made a huge lump in my throat.

Then Kelsey came around, a young girl who we met through 4-H. She had joined the club but didn't own a horse. We offered to let her borrow one of ours for the mounted events and she fell in love with TC as quickly as I did. After their first ride together Kelsey dismounted and wrapped her arms around TC's neck, I opened my mouth to explain that TC didn't hug when to my utter amazement I witnessed what I'm sure was TC's first hug. I guess she's just been waiting for the right person the whole time.

Kelsey's parent purchased TC for Kelsey's birthday as a surprise. I remember the look of surprise and delight on her face when she realized that TC was all hers. I couldn't help but wonder at the irony of it all, TC was one of my favorites horses of all time and the only one I never shed a single tear over selling. I just knew that she had found the perfect home.

I continued to receive updates on how TC was doing for years to come; I got to go visit her, and I even got to introduce my husband to her during the last visit.

Then one day I received a message from Kelsey letting me know that TC had passed away. I took the news harder than I expected, considering that it had been almost ten years since she had really been "my girl." But I still felt an incredible sense of loss, all the fun times we had together came crashing back.

I couldn't help but wonder yet again if heaven will have horses? When I was a little girl my mother assured me that horses would be in heaven because it couldn't be heaven without horses.

As an adult, I've pondered this question a lot, and to be honest I have no idea what the real answer is. The closest thing to an answer that I've found is in Revelations 19:11, "Then I saw heaven opened, and behold, a white horse! The one sitting on it is called Faithful and True, and in righteousness, he judges and makes war."

So we do know that there will be at least *one* horse in heaven. We also know that heaven will be a wonderful place where we will lack nothing and be fully satisfied, with or without horses!

"Heaven is where all the horses you ever loved come to greet you."

The Emergency Brake

As much as I love horses, it is important to remember that a horse is still a fifteen hundred pound animal that can kill you at almost any given moment. Horseback riding is an extreme sport and at any time there is the potential for things to go wrong in a deadly way.

Imagine for a second being on a runaway horse, I've been there and trust me, it is NOT fun. You have a few options to choose from.

1. Go along for the ride. As Grandpa always said, "I can ride as fast as they can run." Not necessarily safe as you basically have no idea how the ride will end. Hint: DUCK when you see a tree branch!
2. Pull back on the reins. Sounds like it should help but if the horse is truly running away they just clamp down on the bit and keep running. This usually scares them more which can cause other behaviors such as bucking or rearing, which is basically the only thing more dangerous than running away.
3. Employ the emergency brake.

Yes, that is correct, horses have emergency brakes. It's quite simple really, you pull their nose around to touch your toe. It doesn't stop them from running, but when they are running they can only go in circles, and not terribly fast ones at that.

Also, because their spine is bent they can't buck or rear, and kicking won't get them anywhere when you're up top.

Horses don't just naturally let you pull their head around to your toe; it's something that you have to teach them right from day one.

When I get a young horse I will slip a halter and rope onto them, and then just give a gentle pressure to the side. They will usually toss their head and dance around for a bit before they realize what I am asking them to do, then they will relax and let me have their head. As soon as they do that I release the pressure and give it back to them. I repeat this exercise literally hundreds of times before I mount a young horse for the first time. I want the response of giving their head to me to be so natural that even if having me on top of their back scares them to death they will still give their heads to me.

Eventually, I will become more insistent and ask them to "give their heads to me" for longer periods of time. I always find it odd how every horse does the same thing. I will pick up on the rope and they will immediately and flawlessly turn their heads, leave it there for a fraction of a second and then yank it back. I need them to leave it there for a period of time or else my emergency brake would only be an emergency pause.

It reminds me of what I sometimes do with God's will. I will sense God coming alongside me, gently placing His hand on my shoulder and saying "You need to do this for me." I'll feel overwhelmed by His love, by His presence, by who He is. I'll drop to my knees and say "Yes! Yes! I will do anything for you!"

But the next day I will begin to worry, I'll remember things like how busy I am, how much I have already done or given and sometimes I'll talk my way out of doing God's perfect will.

The secret is to keep your eyes on God, and remain flexible and open to His will for you because we all need an emergency brake!

First Ride Jitters

I have another horse that I am training (I know what you're thinking, ANOTHER one?! This girl needs some kind of therapy.) She's a stunning Percheron/Arab cross and she's been an absolute sweetheart to work with. She's taller than any of the other horses I've worked with, checking in at sixteen hands high. (Horses are measured at the base of their necks in units known as hands. A hand is equal to four inches. Don't ask me why. I didn't make the rules.)

To be honest her size intimidates me . . . a lot. I usually don't worry about a horse stepping on my toes, but when her hooves are the size of a dinner plate I'm a lot more careful. But that's nothing compared to the problems I have just getting on her.

Typically when I mount a horse the first few times I'll put one foot in the stirrup and pull myself up, but I will just hang there instead of swinging my leg over to sit in the saddle. This allows the horse to get used to seeing me above them as well as allowing me to swiftly dismount and land on my feet if I need to.

But with this mare getting my foot as high as the stirrup is no small feat. To make a long story short when I finally got my foot high enough to reach the stirrup I stuck it in and just swung my leg right over because frankly I wasn't convinced that my foot would ever get that high ever again.

Then I prayed, hard and fast and made soothing sounds to the horse, because even after all of the horses I've got the chance to start, I'm still terrified of the first few rides.

You see it takes faith to get on a horse, a LOT of faith. I need faith in myself for starters. Faith that I will know what to do and be calm enough to do it in case things go south. I need faith in my horse. Faith that they are ready for me to do this, that they can be trusted and will remember their training if they get scared.

But most of all I need faith in God. Because I know beyond a shadow of a doubt that nothing can happen to me that is outside of his will. He has a plan for my life, and I know that His plans are always best.

So if His plan is for me to be in a hospital, or to have a perfect first ride it doesn't matter because no matter what "all things work together for the good of those who love God and are called according to His will." Romans 8:28

Oh, and just in case you were wondering our first ride went perfectly and I couldn't be happier with my mare. Now I'm off to do some flexibility training so I'll be ready for the second ride!

?

ARE YOU A THOROUGHBRED OR A PONY?

There are probably thousands of horse breeds. Each breed has been carefully refined over the years to serve a different purpose.

For instance, the Shire is the biggest breed of horse; they were the semis of the 1800's. By contrast, the Welsh pony is short and stout, carefully bred to be able to fit into small mine shafts and pull large weights. Arabians are the oldest breed; they were prized by dessert nomads for their endurance and beauty. Quarter Horses were developed as working cow horses and tend to have short legs and a stocky frame allowing them to turn sharp and quick. Thoroughbreds have been used mainly as race horses and are lean and tall. I could go on and on, each breed is carefully fine-tuned for a specific purpose.

Have you ever wondered what your purpose is? I think every human being has wondered exactly that at some point in their life.

If we believe in a loving God who sacrificed Himself for us, then we have to believe that He did that for a reason. God has given each of us talents and gifts.

Some of them are obvious, the ones with beautiful voices, the concert pianist, the eloquent speakers.

Some are not so obvious, the prayer warriors, the patient Sunday school teacher, or the person who can make anyone feel welcome.

Often Satan undermines our gifts by attacking our self-confidence. He loves to whisper lies, "You can't sing in church, you're voice isn't that good." Or "You're not really good with children; remember the time you were watching little Johnny and he got a bruise?" Often we will believe his lies and tell ourselves that we are just being humble. But THEY ARE LIES!

Psalm 139:13 tells us that before God knit us in our mother's wombs He knew us. If you are breathing, God has a plan and a purpose for your life.

Chase that plan! Seek it, pray about it, stop at nothing to find out what it is.

A good horse breeding program can produce amazing qualities, but even with all our technology we still can't select the features that the offspring will produce. But God can. You were created with just the right features to serve God, so go serve Him.

⁇

Riding Side Way

Some parts of training a horse are really easy. For instance, the basic idea of round penning is based on how a wild horse herd functions. So when you first put a horse in a round pen it doesn't take very long at all for them to catch on to what you are trying to do with them.

The same is true when you ride a horse for the first time. You climb on and if you are lucky and the horse is accepting of you on their back it doesn't take long to learn walk, stop, left and right. These are things that horses naturally do in the pasture.

But some things are not so easy, for instance teaching a horse to side pass. Side passing as the name implies involves the horse walking sideways. A proper side pass involves the horse stepping their front legs across each other. It may seem like a useless thing to teach a horse at first, but when you need to do something like close a gate or get your horse out of a dangerous situation it can come in really handy.

This is the situation I found myself in with my black Arabian mare one afternoon. It's not an easy thing to teach a horse because in order to get motion in the horse you have to put some leg pressure on them. Up until that point in their training leg pressure has always meant one thing, move forward. So the horse moves forward and the rider stops them, still keeping the leg pressure on their side.

As you can well imagine a horse can get extremely frustrated really quickly this way. To help my horses figure out the puzzle I will typically line them up with a wall or fence and apply leg pressure. It still frustrates them (they probably think that their rider just lost her marbles) but they tend to figure it out quicker and without as much pressure.

It's a tricky situation to be in as a trainer also. Some horses try going forward, backward, forward, backward and then in frustration they just stop and ignore all pressure. Or some horses will try other methods of expressing their frustration, tossing their heads, pawing the ground, shaking their heads . . . but eventually, they all seem to do the same thing, give up and decide to ignore the pressure.

I have learned through trial and error that the best way to handle this situation is to just keep gently applying pressure until the horse moves again. At that point, I don't care which direction the move, just as long as they move a foot I immediately take the pressure off and let them rest.

The lesson that I'm trying to enforce is no longer "move your feet sideways" but "move your feet when you feel leg pressure."

I wonder how often God has tried to teach me the same lesson? So often I have gotten frustrated and angry and said "God, I don't see where this road that you have me on is going, so I'm just going to sit in front of my TV until you fill me in." and drown Him out with the noise of everyday life.

And so often He's come beside me, gently tapped me on the shoulder and just kept tapping until He finally got me up off the couch and back moving my proverbial feet.

At the end of the day, we might not understand exactly why God put us in certain situations or exactly why this or that uncomfortable thing had to happen to us. But in Jeremiah 29:11 we are told, "For I know the plans I have for you," says the Lord . "They are plans for good and not for disaster, to give you a future and a hope. God works all things together for the good of those who love Him and are called according to His will."

So sometimes even if you're not one hundred percent sure where He's leading you, just keep trusting and just keep moving your feet. You never know, He might even want you to go sideways!

?

Isolated Lessons

Over the years I have learned that it is actually possible to speed up how quickly a horse learns. It has come in handy when I'm starting young horses and would like to take them on a particular trail ride or to a show that is coming up soon.

They are actually pretty basic things, like making sure that the horse is healthy, in good shape, well fed, has the proper minerals, fresh water, etc. But one of my secrets is a little unexpected.

Often when you are riding a horse daily you will seem to spend the first half of your session repeating what you did during the last session, unless you employ my sneaky little shortcut to fast horse training. If you do this one trick you will often be able to cut your training time by about one third.

I know I'm beginning to sound like I'm selling the latest weight loss product, but I really have had good success with this.

When I am finished riding the horse that I am training, I place them in either a box stall or a pen by themselves until the next session. It's a trick from my mother and believe it or not it works really well.

My theory (although not scientifically proven) is that the time alone gives the horse a chance to think about what you did with them. In fact, often when I do this I find that the horse works better the following day then they did during their last training session. It's almost as though they stand in their pen and slowly it dawns on them what you were trying to teach them.

There's something about being alone that just seems to slow the world down and everything begins to make sense again.

Now don't get me wrong, I'm not saying that we should avoid other people, in fact just the opposite, the Bible commands us to fellowship with other believers, but there is definitely a time and place when it is more than appropriate to just be alone with God and meditate on who He is and what He has done for us.

Life is constantly trying to distract us from this with television, cell phones, laptops and rush hours. In fact, sometimes it is our well-intended church activities that distract us.

We become so busy teaching Sunday school, helping out with the youth group or practicing with the worship team that we forget about the very God that we are allegedly serving.

1 Samuel 15:22 says, "Then Samuel said, "Does the LORD take pleasure in burnt offerings and sacrifices as much as he does in obedience? Certainly, obedience is better than sacrifice; paying attention is better than the fat of rams."

God would rather have us stop and pay attention to Him then run around in a wild frenzy attempting to "do His work." God is more than capable of making sure that His work gets done.

So take some time today to stop, to just be still and know that He is God. You will learn life's lessons much faster if you do.

THE FALL

After my husband and I had been married for a few months, a remarkable circumstance led us to purchase two five-year-old warmblood horses.

I decided to focus most of my training on the smaller of the two geldings, a tall reddish brown horse whom we dubbed Autumn Dreamer. (note: my horse friends teased me endlessly about that name. Apparently, my horse names are quite flowery.)

Although Autumn came along quite well in his training it soon became obvious that he wasn't a horse whom I would be keeping. At the time I wanted a nice quite mount that I could use for trail riding with my husband and friends, although Autumn was compliant, he was clearly bred to be a jumper and more on the skittish side than what I was looking for.

After I had about ten rides on him I decided to go ahead and post an ad for him on a local website. Shortly after a woman called me up and asked to come view him.

Up until that point, my rides on Autumn had been really, really basic. Mainly I was just happy if I could sit on him and get him to move around while relaxed. The main obstacle to that had been how "herd bound" Autumn was. (Herd bound is a term used to describe a horse who grows anxious and or refuses to leave the herd of horses.)

As a result of this, I had been having a really difficult time getting Autumn to walk past the gate to the riding pen. His idea of a ride was me sitting on his back and staring at the gate until I got off.

The day the buyer came to look at Autumn I fussed over him and groomed him perfectly, and after she arrived I put him through his paces in the round pen and finally added a saddle and bridle to the picture.

I closed the gate climbed on and began to show her the basic things I had done with him. To my delight, he was riding better than ever and at one point I was even able to get him to walk straight away from the gate with just the slightest bit of pressure from my legs.

I twisted in my leather saddle and bragged to the buyer, "This is the best he's ever done . . ."

But before I could finish my sentence Autumn turned into a rodeo bronc. He bucked and twisted like no other horse I'd ever been on. I tried to pull him into a small circle to get him to stop bucking and then everything turned into a blur.

The next thing I knew I was lying on the ground unable to breathe with horse hooves raining down all around me and pain shooting throughout my body. I said a quick prayer that this horse wouldn't trample me and tried to roll away from his hooves as my husband, who could see that I had fallen, clear chased the horse away from me. (Rolling was a bad idea and actually increased my chances of getting stepped on so don't do that at home just FYI.)

When all was said and done and I could breathe again, I was black and blue all down my legs and had a crazy sore back but otherwise was no worse for the wear.

My main problem was extreme embarrassment that I had been too busy bragging about my horse and hadn't been paying attention to him.

I couldn't help but relate it to Proverbs 16:18 which says "Pride goes before destruction and haughtiness before a fall."

It was an important lesson to learn and one that I will not soon forget.

PERFECT FEAR

After my unfortunate fall from Autumn, I faced a new problem in riding horses, fear. In fact, I think terror might be a better word for how I felt. I felt just fine when I worked from the ground with a horse, lunging, saddling for the first time, introducing the bit, all of it was no problem. Right up to the point where I placed my foot in the stirrup for the first time.

At that point I felt icy fingers of fear wrap around my heart, my stomach started to churn and sometimes when I was in the saddle I would just begin to freeze, convinced that my horse was about to blow up again.

The mare I was working with at the time was exceptionally sweet and patient with me, and even though she did nothing wrong I continued to fear riding her.

I tried to justify my fear by saying I was just being safety conscious, but after a while, even I couldn't make that excuse work.

My mare at the time was bordering on being too old to train and I knew that if I didn't do something soon she would become useless.

Then one day I was reading and a passage of scripture jumped out that I felt like God had given to me just for this situation.

The verses were Genesis 1:29-29, "Then God said, 'I give you every seed-bearing plant on the face of the whole earth and every tree that has fruit with seed in it. They will be yours for food. And to all the beasts of the earth and all the birds in the sky and all the creatures that move along the ground-- everything that has the breath of life in it--I give every green plant for food.'"

It's funny how you can read the same verse at different stages of your life and get such difference things from it each time. In the past when I had read this verse I hadn't really paid much attention to it, but this time something jumped out at me.

I felt the Holy Spirit impress upon me that He gave me animals as a gift, not something to fear.

But I rationalized, that doesn't mean I have to RIDE one of them, that would be too scary.

What does the Bible say casts out all fear?

Perfect Love (1 John 4:18)

Who loves us perfectly?

God does.

But do we trust him?

And guess what? The next time I got on that horse I was still scared, my stomach still hurt and I still had a hard time breathing.

But I forced myself to take a deep breath and reminded myself that nothing could happen to me that was outside of the will of my heavenly father. After all, a God who sacrificed

His only born son for me wouldn't let a horse bring any harm to me unless He had my ultimate good in mind.

Bravery has nothing to do with not being scared and everything to do with having an all-powerful and always loving God who is always, *always*, with you and has your best interest in hand.

⏷

HORSES AS PROOF THAT GOD LOVES YOU

Just because I managed to get on a horse didn't mean that all my fear was instantly gone. When I put my butt in the saddle suddenly the only thing I could hear was my heart beat.

Since all of the horses I owned at the time were young and barely trained I thought it would be in my best interest to purchase a horse who had been ridden longer and would be a quieter and safer mount for me to use while I tried to get my confidence back.

I searched the internet for horses for sale and discovered that a horse like that was probably going to cost me about $4,000. At best I had $1,500 to spend, and even that seemed like a stretch. I sent up a prayer for the perfect horse to walk into my life, but to be honest I wasn't about to get my hopes up.

Months passed and I continued to watch horse ads, but never found anything that was even close to my price range.

Then one day while I was browsing I happened across a picture of one of the most beautiful horses I had ever seen. She was just a baby and the price was quite cheap so I assumed that she was untrained and not the horse I was looking for.

Still, she was so gorgeous that I took a screenshot of her and sent it to my husband with an expression of my admiration. I never even read the ad.

He texted me right back and said: "let's go look at her". Now I was curious, what about this horse had made him want to go look? I went back and re-read the ad.

She was just a young horse, but she was well started, had been ridden by beginner's and her owner claimed that she was quiet and reliable. Exactly what I had been looking for! Best of all she $800, easily within my budget.

As I sat staring at my phone screen and wondering "could this be my new horse?", an ad came on the TV for the Cadence Law Firm. I never heard an audible voice, but I was overcome with a strong sense of *knowing*. I knew that this would be my new horse and that I would call her Cadence.

Within a week Cadence was living in our pasture, and she was truly the answer to my prayers. She helped me rebuild my confidence and she has been my partner for shows, trail rides and life in general.

There is so much about Cadence that is so perfect for me, she is the perfect height, she is a color and a breed that I have always wanted to own. The funny thing is that her previous owner told me that she was an "accident." That a stallion jumped a fence he wasn't supposed to and the breeding resulted in my Cadence (aka Cadey.)

But there are no accidents. When I see Cadey I see that God loved me enough to create my dream horse and give her to me for half of the budget I had for horse buying. Cadey, just like everybody who ever enters your life is truly a miracle.

There Is Always Enough

Remember when I said that Cadey was the perfect horse for me? Well, that is almost entirely true. The only catch is that Cadey was severely malnourished when I purchased her.

It was so bad that for the first six months that I owned her I had to keep her separate from the other horses and feed her and feed her and feed her. In fact, I couldn't even ride her for the first three months.

Her ribs protruded, her hips protruded and her eyes bulged out. Her hooves hadn't been trimmed and she was a scraggly sight that warmed your heart and broke it simultaneously.

Every time I went out to feed her she would go a little crazy. She even knocked me over to get to hay or grain. Trying to lead her over grass was extremely difficult because her nose would be glued to the ground. I jokingly called her "my bulldozer" and "my lawnmower" but it wasn't really funny.

I honestly thought that after I had owned her for a while and she realized that there was plenty of hay and grain in her new home that she would calm down around food. But it turns out that wasn't true.

With time and training she became respectful and is no longer a bulldozer and a lawnmower, but she is still panicked around food. If I put a large bale in her pen she will stand and eat until it is ALL gone. Most horses will eat until they are full and then come back, but not Cadey. I have to constantly manage her weight or she will get so fat that it is unhealthy.

Over and over I have explained to her that I like her and intend to feed her well, but apparently, her English isn't the best. I now consider it a cute, but sad quirk that she will most likely carry with her for life, and I can't help but think how I do this in my life too.

My whole life I have always had enough money. At times it hasn't felt like enough, but I have lived to this point, so obviously I got by. Yet how often do I hear myself asking God for more, or worrying about the bills?

I'm really no different than Cadey with her head buried in a hay bale and her sides bulging out. And I'm sure that God loves and intends to care for me even more than I love and intend to care for Cadey. So we can relax, because there will be enough hay and money, there is always enough.

[?]

BLACKIE CANNOT TELL A LIE

I love going to look at horses for sale, even when I cannot afford to buy them and have no intention of doing so. If I have a friend, or a friend's cousin, or a friend's cousin's uncle, I will beg to go horse shopping with them.

Why? Simple, because horses don't lie and people often do.

Take for example the time I went with one of my friends to look at a horse known as "Blackie." My friend was interested in purchasing a horse for a camp she volunteered at and invited me to come along and offer my opinion; of course, I jumped at the opportunity!

She had discovered the advertisement buried in the classified section of our small town's newspaper. A short black and white paragraphed offered two sentences and a price.

"For sale, 10-year-old QH gelding, 14'2 hands high. Used in the rodeo $1,200obo"

(Translation 10-year-old smallish horse bred to chase cows, used in the rodeo asking $1,200 or best offer.)

I read it and immediately laughed, then asked sarcastically "What was he used in the rodeo for? A bucking bronc?" Rodeo is a complex sport with about one hundred different uses for a horse, so the words "used" in a rodeo are extremely vague.

My friend had already called the attached phone number and armed with some vague directions and a cell phone we were off like a herd of turtles. Forty-five minutes, three wrong turns, and two phone calls later we arrived at our destination. A small yard in a village, barely big enough to keep a horse. The pasture was crudely fenced with wire and right beside the landowner's trailer home.

As soon as we stepped out of the truck we were surrounded by about ten neighborhood children. They excitedly began asking us all kinds of questions.

"Are you here to buy Blackie?" A little blonde girl queried.

"Blackie bucked me off!" A young boy with brown eyes announced as he proudly thrust out his chest.

"He bucked me off too!" This one looked like the little girl's brother.

"He did not buck you off! You fell off!" It looked like a fight was about to break out.

The whole time a fortyish couple was trying desperately to shut the children up. They quickly shooed them off the yard and reduced the number to three blonde-haired blue-eyed children who clearly belonged to them.

We were ushered into the pasture where we met Blackie. First glance informed me that he was clearly NOT a quarter horse and he was a solid six to eight inches taller than the ad had claimed.

The owners proudly reminded us that he had been used in the Calgary Stampede, but when pressed for more details they had no idea if he had been used for roping, or barrels, or a bucking bronc, or the petting zoo.

89

They tied Blackie to the bumper of a rusting truck which was rotting in the middle of their pasture (please don't try this at home, a large horse can easily pull a truck wherever they choose) and produced one of the most tattered and worn saddles I had ever seen in my life. After which they placed the oldest of their blonde children on the back of the horse.

I couldn't help but notice that the little boy was hesitant to climb on, and as soon as he was situated in the saddle he grasped the horn of the saddle with both hands and hung on with a look of sheer terror in his eyes.

His parents led Blackie with the eldest son in tow in a circle of about a ten-foot diameter, the whole time Blackie had his ears pinned back and his back hunched, looking at the world like he was about to explode into a bucking fit. When they stopped, the little boy dove from the horse's back as quickly as possible, then he fist pumped the air turned and announced "See? You can ride him!"

Apparently, our definition of riding was a little bit different than his, this horse was clearly not safe for children and possibly not safe for adults!

The owners spent the next hour trying to convince us that Blackie was a very quiet, well-mannered kid's horse, perfectly suited for use at a camp with a bunch of beginner riders. To be fair I don't think they were purposefully lying, I think they honestly believed that.

But no matter how well spoken and convincing they were, one look at Blackie's body language when he was being ridden told me that he wasn't anywhere near as quiet as these people believed he was.

It reminded me of the lies we often tell God and ourselves. Lies like, " I won't read my Bible today, but tomorrow I'll read for twice as long as usual so it's ok."

Or "I will start tithing with my *next* paycheck, not this one"

But at the end of the day even if we can fool ourselves we can't fool God. He created us and knows us better than anyone else, so why do we try so hard to keep up appearances with Him? Why not just be honest, after all, He knows the truth anyway.

⁇

LOPING WITH CADENCE

Horseback riding is considered an extreme sport, which is odd to me since I love horseback riding and I'm basically the most unextreme person ever.

That is the reason after owning my mare Cadence (aka Cadey) for over a year, we still hadn't spent much time loping. (Loping, by the way, is when the horse is running not quite flat out.)

The other part of the reason is because Cadey is naturally a bit of a slow mover and she prefers taking naps and eating hay to running in circles. Instead of loping we worked on creating a nice headset and improving her trot (a slower gait were horses simply jog), learning to stand quietly, and backing up nicely.

Finally one crisp fall afternoon I decided that I couldn't procrastinate any longer, so I took Cadey out to a nice open field and began to ask for a nice lope.

At first, Cadey refused, but after I insisted for a while she offered up a few steps and then refused again. This went on for a period of time and then "it" happened.

Cadey began to offer up every trick I had ever taught her, she backed beautifully, stood like a statue and tucked her head into the ideal location. ALL without me even ASKING!

I realized what she was doing. This was her way of getting out of having to lope. All these other things were easier for her to do than loping, so she was giving me one after the other to distract me from the hard thing.

Isn't that exactly what we do sometimes? "Okay God, I'll give you church on Sunday and volunteering with the youth group, but don't bring up my TV show that is my guilty pleasure."

And just like Cadey couldn't fool me for a second, we're not fooling God either.

⁇

THE THINGS MY HORSES WON'T DO

Let's say that you're in the market for a horse for your son or daughter. There are certain characteristics that you would look for.

You want your child to be safe so it is important that the horse would not scare easily, you also want a horse that doesn't buck, rear, run away, kick, or bite.

Now let's say that you find a horse who is perfectly safe, he doesn't buck, rear, run away, kick, or bite. BUT when you put your child on him he simply does *nothing.*

Despite the rider's best efforts to get the horse to walk, trot, lope, or back, the horse just stands like a statue. Would you buy that horse? Is that horse worth anything to you?

More importantly, does this behavior describe your faith? I have met a lot of Christians (unfortunately I could be included in this group) who are very proud that they don't smoke, drink, do drugs, swear, or work on Sunday. But those things don't make you any more useful than a horse who stands in the middle of the ring and refuses to move.

Being a Christian should be about all the things that you are doing, not about all the things that you are *not* doing.

It is so important to honor your conscience and the still small voice of God that whispers to your soul when He is telling you *not* to do something.

BUT it is also important to honor that still small voice of God when he is telling you to go do something.

94

What is it that God is telling you to do?

ABOUT THE AUTHOR

Kayla Peters is an animal loving writer who lives and ranches in Canada with her husband Tim. She wasn't born in a barn but she went there as fast as she could.

OTHER BOOKS KAYLA PETERS

Tales From The Table

Booked Up!

The Chocolate Lover`s Cookbook

ONE LAST THING

If you enjoyed this book or found it useful I'd be very grateful if you'd post a short review on Amazon. Your support really does make a difference and I read all the reviews personally so I can get your feedback and make this book even better.

Sometimes Kayla Peters gives away books for FREE, but these promotions are for a very limited time. If you would like to be notified when Kayla is giving away a free book click this link.

Made in the USA
San Bernardino, CA
22 August 2019